'Twas the Night B'fore Christmas

The Weathersby's Christmas Eve 1904

'Twas the Night B'fore Christmas

An African-American Version

Retold and Illustrated by Melodye Rosales

Based on the original poem
A Visit From St. Nicholas
by Clement C. Moore

SCHOLASTIC INC.
New York Toronto London Auckland Sydney

'Twas the night b'fore Christmas,
   when all 'round the house,
Not a critter was stirrin',
   not even a mouse.
The stockin's were laid
   by the chimney wit' care,
For the chil'ren hoped Santy Claus
   soon would be there.

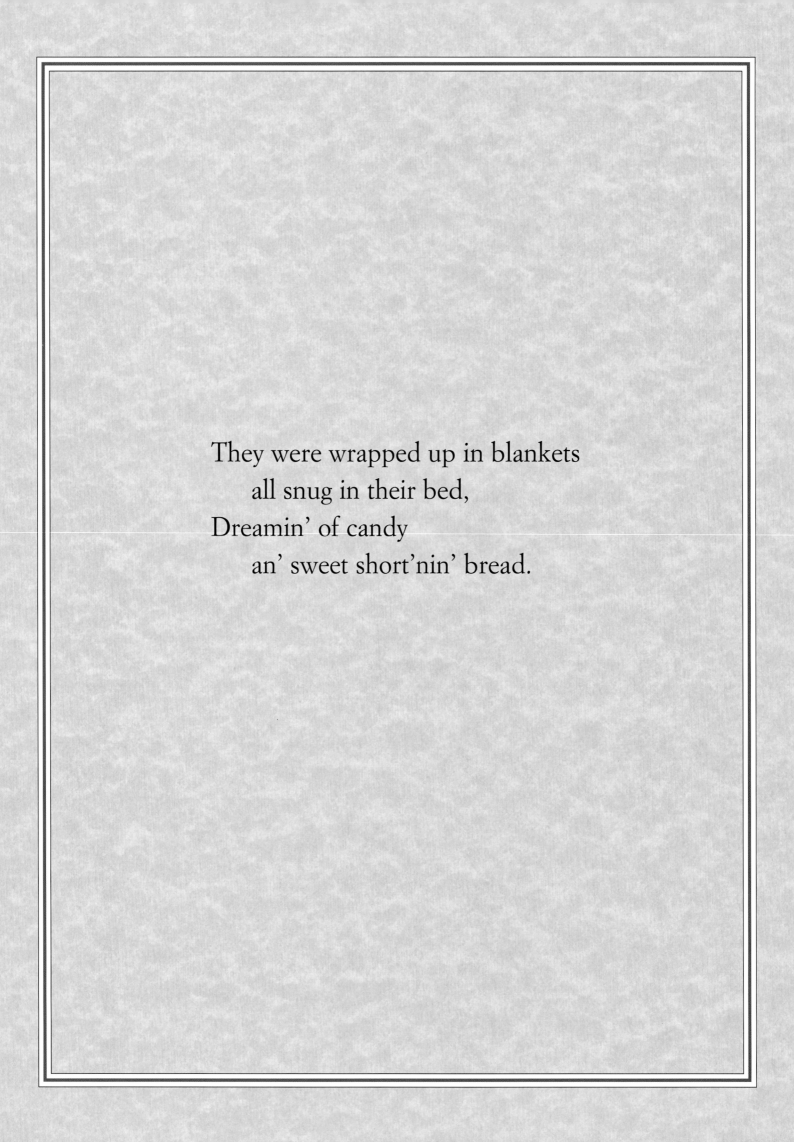

They were wrapped up in blankets
   all snug in their bed,
Dreamin' of candy
   an' sweet short'nin' bread.

Wit' me in my flannels
    an' Ma in her cap,
We'd jus' bedded down
    for a long winter's nap.

When outta the darkness
        there came such a clatter,
Made me jump from my bed
        to see what was the matter.

To the window I flew
 in a jackrabbit dash,
An' snatched back the curtains
 as quick as a flash.
The moonlight shone 'top
 of the ol' wooden shed,
Blindin' my eyes
 as it sparkled an' spread.

Then all of a sudden—
   I saw it real clear—
Came a thimble-sized sled
   wit' eight tiny reindeer,
An' a li'l' ol' driver
   so spry an' so quick,
It come to me direc'ly,
   "Why, that's ol' St. Nick!"

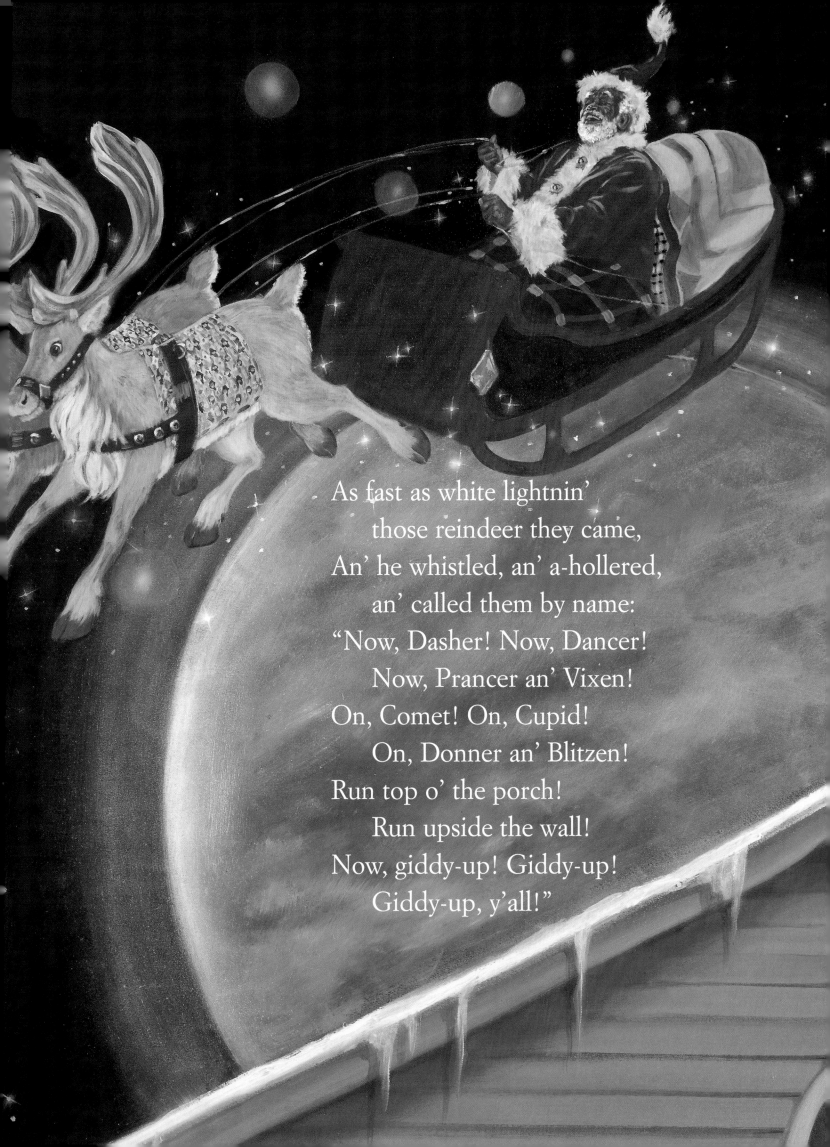

As fast as white lightnin'
    those reindeer they came,
An' he whistled, an' a-hollered,
    an' called them by name:
"Now, Dasher! Now, Dancer!
    Now, Prancer an' Vixen!
On, Comet! On, Cupid!
    On, Donner an' Blitzen!
Run top o' the porch!
    Run upside the wall!
Now, giddy-up! Giddy-up!
    Giddy-up, y'all!"

Like tobacco leaves whipped
    by a hurricane fly,
Like the four winds that meet
    'fore they jump to the sky,
On up to the rooftop
    them reindeer they flew,
Wit' a passel of goodies
    an' Santy Claus, too.
In a lickety-split I heard
    up on the roof,
The struttin' an' steppin'
    of each li'l' hoof.

As I pulled in my head
     an' had turnt myself 'round,
Glory be! Down the chimney
     he came wit' a bound!
His getup had possum fur,
     head clear to foot,
An' his suit was all blackened
     wit' ashes an' soot.
A big quilt-wrapped bundle
     he'd flung 'cross his back,
An' he looked like a conjure man
     openin' his sack.

Oh, my! How his eyes shone
    like coals lit white hot!
His cheeks puffed like bread puddin'
    baked in a pot.
Wit' his cotton-white hair
    peekin' out from his cap,
An' skin like molasses,
    he looked jus' like my Pap!
He was jumpin', an' a-hoppin'—
    doin' the pigeonwing—
An' I tried not to laugh
    when he started to sing.
An ol' corncob pipe
    he gripped tight 'twixt his teeth,
An' smoke circled his head
    like a Georgia pine wreath.

Wit' a wink of his eye
    an' a nod of his head,
He gave me to know
    that I need not be 'fraid.
He went 'bout his business,
    kep' straight at his work,
Stuffed all them stockin's,
    then turnt 'round wit' a jerk.

Whilst layin' a finger
      alongside his nose,
Wit' nary a word
      up the chimney he rose.

He jumped on his sled,
    gave his reindeer a holler,
An' away they all flew
    like a hard-earnt dollar.
Then I heard him shout back
    when he got outta sight,

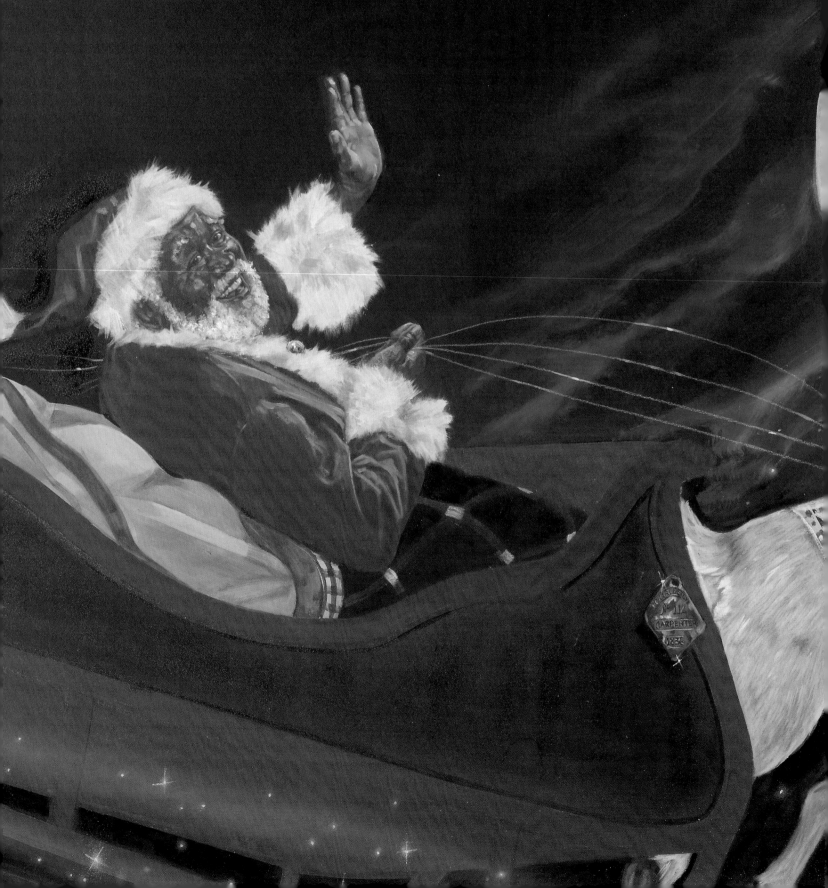

"Merry Christmas To All!
Y'all Sleep Tight!"

In memory of Reverend Earl Kennedy
1918–1995
affectionately known as the "waving pastor," who stood in front of his church many
mornings and evenings calling out to those passing by, often complete strangers:
"Have a good day!" or "God bless you!"
…a real Santa Claus who devoted his time and energy every Christmas to bringing magic
to children who are often forgotten—children-at-risk.

Acknowledgments

To my editor, Bernette Ford, thank you for entrusting me to bring your vision to reality
To my art director, Edie Weinberg, thank you for allowing me to create
To my sister, Kaye Benson, my writing mentor, without whom I could not have
done this book, and my brother, Chris Benson, for always listening and
giving me constructive criticism

Special thanks to Professor William E. Berry; Professor Violet J. Harris; Bruce Nesbitt,
Director, Afro-American Cultural Center; and Ronald Claibourne, all affiliated with
University of Illinois-Urbana-Champaign

To my family, who always patiently wait for me to finish painting so they can give me needed
hugs and kisses: Giraldo, Giraldo Jr., Harmony, and Symphony

Library of Congress Cataloging-in-Publication Data

Rosales, Melodye.
    'Twas the night b'fore Christmas / retold and illustrated by Melodye Rosales.
      p. cm.
    "An African-American version based on the original poem, A visit from St. Nicholas, by Clement C. Moore."
    Summary: Presents a turn-of-the-century black family's encounter with St. Nick as he delivers his presents before flying
  off into the night.
    ISBN 0-590-73944-1
    1. Afro-American families—Juvenile poetry.   2. Santa Claus—Juvenile poetry.   3. Christmas—Juvenile poetry.   4.
Children's poetry, American.   [1. Afro-Americans—Poetry.   2. Santa Claus—Poetry.   3. Christmas—Poetry. 4. American
poetry. 5. Narrative poetry.]   I. Moore, Clement Clarke, 1779-1863.   Night before Christmas.   II. Title.
PS3568.0738T93   1996
811'.54—dc20   95-53236
                                                                                                                                       CIP
                                                                                                                                       AC

12 11 10 9 8 7 6 5 4 3 2 1   6 7 8 9/9 0 1/0
                              Printed in Singapore
                        First Scholastic printing, October 1996